Common Sense, Too.

Are you still in my pew?

Copyright 2016

God and the Bible
Politically incorrect

Why do we hang onto the old views anddiscriminations that pull everyone apart? Should we believe in a God that is neither tolerant nor accepting to the way life is at this moment? Shouldn't He change instead of us? Should the Bible dictate what we can or cannot do? This is the modern thought of a world that prefers evil over good. How do we satisfy this yearning to be the worst rather than the best?

We thank God when everything goes right and damn Him when we don't get our way. Should we change scripture to make it say what we want it to say? Many favor abortion and gay marriage, so should we edit the Bible to make it more user-friendly. Let's start with the Ten Commandments which are obviously politically incorrect.

The first commandment says that we should not have any other gods before us. Is that fair to all other gods? Men and women have made all kind of idol-gods and freely worship them. That is clearly discriminatory and we should really eliminate that particular commandment. If we are to be fair and politically correct we need to scratch off the first commandment.

Why should Allah, Buddha. etc. be taken out of any faith because God says so? Modern society should be allowed to worship the moon, the stars, stone monuments or a candy bar without the wrath of any intolerant God. So who does God think He is by telling us who we should worship? So scratch that commandment.

The second commandment talks about making graven images. Well-l-l-l, let's see since He is now taking away artistic creativity and finding a spiritual awakening in the work that was formed by human hands, shouldn't we expunge the symbol of the Cross? Shouldn't we accept the image of Satan whose image is an alternative to God? What is the harm of this kind of creativity? We cannot tolerate this infringement on free will. Didn't He give us that choice and why should we be punished by exercising that free will? Scratch number two.

Next is the third commandment of using the name of the Lord in vain. No, that is a violation of our freedom of speech. We must be able to express ourselves in whatever language we choose. Isn't that a right of verbal freedom? Maybe we don't mean it as a slight to God, but just a moment of anguish or anger. Doesn't God forgive everything we do or say? Many churches make excuses to keep their pews full. So scratch that one off, too.

The fourth commandment violates our right to work. The Sabbath day may be assigned to a day of rest, but who can? God has no bills to pay so He doesn't understand the needs of the family. Employers do not see the need for their workers to rest because it hurts the bottom line. All that overtime might go to waste and we are sure God does not want us to waste our time. Another one bites the dust.

Thou shall not kill, the fifth commandment, but abortion is legal, self-defense is necessary and war is inevitable so another commandment goes by the wayside. Which brings us to the reason for abortion in the next commandment which is do not commit adultery. Aren't there reasons for adultery? Excuses for infidelity? My husband/wife doesn't understand me. My husband/wife is not interested in me. God has to understand our needs. Isn't He a bachelor?

Also the tenth commandment about coveting your neighbor's wife must be eliminated since we come back to abortion and the fifth commandment to hide the sin. Is it our fault we find women or men attractive? Isn't that new car of our neighbor's incredible? What wouldn't we do to be successful and have nice things. Doesn't God want the best for us? A somewhat useless commandment if God wants us to succeed in life and help fill the coffers of the church.

So now we have the great four commandments. Life will be easier and less guilty with fewer commandments. We've cut down on our commitment of the Constitution, so why not God's laws?

Gay marriage nullifies several scripture passages such as Lev., II Timothy, Corinthians. Abortion dictates to us that we must erase several passages to update the moral obligations of the present age. What else can we find that we can lessen the burden of reading such an overwhelming book that castrates our freedoms to do as we please? Why not just have a handbook of a hundred pages or less?

Why do we believe that God is an inhibitor of a good life? Is it the cases of VD? A.I.D.S.? Unwanted pregnancies? Moral decay? Divorce? Which everyone knows is a good thing to have. Why would we want a true definition between right and wrong? Are we fools because we follow Christ, our Lord? Where is the honor if we do the right thing? What is the merit to weakly live our lives and sit on thrones of stone? Thousands have died these past two years for saying "As for me and my family, I will follow the Lord." Young children are beheaded because they said they will follow Jesus not Mohammed. Are we strong enough to look death in the eye and say "Take me for I go to a better place?"

What is the purpose of life if we do not live it without purpose? Are we only dust where nothing but darkness and oblivion awaits us? We are fools believing that life is an accident. Do we not inherently know right from wrong and choose to do what we want? We go to church, but many times the Lord is left behind. Whether we want to or not we fear God and through that fear we decide to defy Him or worship Him. How do we really know except through scripture and history the reality of our God? There is no doubt He exists except the doubt we want to think is there. We fear because we refuse to understand the meaning of our lives. To serve God is cowardice to many people because we have to rely on someone besides ourselves. We think therefore we are, but when God thinks we will always be.

As one gets older, we think we know better

before we find out we learned nothing. We believe money and power are the only things that turned to dust not the souls of men. Until we learn differently, God cannot be reached in prayer. Without faith, nothing can be learned or taught. Without faith, there is no purpose in life. Without faith, who do we answer to if there is nothing there who will respond to us? Why do we not have chaos in the universe or the natural world? Chaos is man-made and self-destruction comes from the evil that opposes God. When we use the name Satan, we think of horror movies not the subtle creature we think is red with a tail and horns. Actually Satan is a magnificent creature, handsome to see and deceptive in all the vices mankind craves for.

> "And no wonder, for Satan himself masquerades as an angel of light"
>
> II Corinthians 11:14

The horror of Satan is when the individual

realizes he has been deceived while he stands before God and then it is too late. Living a good life will not get you to heaven nor will giving to charities add brownie points to open the gate. Why is it easier to follow Satan then God? Because consuming passions feel good. It is easier to stage war than peace. It is easier to take than work for it. Multiple partners are better than marriage. Lying is more of a defense then to tell the truth and take the consequences of one's actions. To take a life than to save it. To deny God than to praise Him. To add another nail to the cross than to kneel before it. To listen to an echo from the empty tomb than to wonder about the voice that came from it. To blame others than to take responsibility. To hate than to love.

Who stands to gain from all this? God is perfect in forgiveness and judgment while we look around for an exit, hoping we won't be seen. Where do we hide?

It is easier to defend one's country from the enemy without. It is far worse to defend our country if we ourselves are the enemy. If we forsake the

Constitution who will stand for it? If we renege on our freedom, who will be free? If our faith in God becomes suspect, who will resurrect it? Why care about death if there are no consequences after death? What good are moral rules if no one cares about morals? If we believe God is dead, so are we.

Chapter Two

I'LL Take My Nation Hyphenated

The real problem with America is that we have become a hyphenated people. It's like decaffeinated coffee. Neither is richer or fuller in taste because the very soul has been taken out.

The church has lost its taste, it's vigor for filling pews and gathering tithes and offerings has been a means to waylay the message. The words are watered down to be politically correct so as not to disturb the status quo. Did not Jesus disturb the status quo? Was he politically correct using hyphenated statements to ease the message?

Before I get into the hyphenated message that tears apart our country, I wish to write about the Christians slaughtered all over the world. Children are beheaded because they will not deny Jesus. Here in the United States we are denying our faith. We have become like frogs in tepid water while the fires burn beneath us until we boil to death.

Who dares speak out about the inequality, injustice and immorality that is that boiling water? Few listen to the cries of injustice though those who cry out excuse their actions with rifles and bombs. Christians have changed their vision to be included with society rather than be different and set examples.

Does anyone believe our division using hyphens will subside as taxes go higher, medical care becomes overwhelming and churches close their self-interested eyes permanently hoping the government won't shut them down?

Business taxes rise to 38% pushing jobs and

companies overseas. Personal taxes rise to 40% or more for state and nation as a punishment for being successful. $15 an hour minimum is supposed to help those at the bottom of the ladder, but instead will add to the unemployed. More regulations make fewer companies appear to hire those unemployed.

What has this to do with hyphenated America? Because certain groups of society are ignored for the few lucky ones to have jobs. The media bears the brunt of this prejudice as they show ever more black faces in crime. Low income white individuals robbing and fighting because they have little else to do are put on the back pages.

What is the answer? Seek Jesus in churches? Jesus who? The churches reportedly are more interested in filling pews and offering plates than preaching faith, sacrifice and martyrdom. Who wants to be one of those in the Middle East to be beheaded for Christ? How many would be willing to denounce Christ than be beheaded?

One more thing before I get to the true topic of

this chapter. Where is the courage to stand up to politicians who circumvent the law, pass immoral edicts and refuse to remember our past, our Constitution and our Declaration of Independence?

We divided ourselves into a hyphenated society that refuses to have peace and understanding because of past wrongs living in the past and blaming those who weren't there only fans the flames of hatred.

This country will never be perfect, but compared to any other nation we are the last bastion of life, liberty and the pursuit of happiness. Where else can an individual be allowed to become whatever he is willing to work to be? He can use his voice to make his opinions openly known and change the course of history as is his right. We have the right not to listen if we disagree without killing each other.

Now this is where there has been a change in America. We are no longer just Americans. We are hyphenated Americans who want justice for only our group and no other. Protest if you must, but violence and killing destroys the message. No one listens when people die or are maimed on either side. Where else can you protest and be heard? Most countries help you disappear than give you a podium to speak your mind.

Yes, we have a free press, but it is slowly being taken over by billionaires who dictate what is to be believed or misshapes the truth. The truth is out there, find it.

Crying out that you are Afro-American, does that mean you are from Africa and have a connection with America? If you cry out that you are White-American, does that give you special privileges or are you European with ties to America? If you cry out you are Latin-American, does that mean you are from South America with ties to America? If you are Asian-American, does that mean you are from China or Japan with a connection to America?

I do not see anything in the Declaration of Independence that says we are hyphenated Americans. The phrase in particular reads "We hold these truths to be self-evident, that all men are created equal" not hyphenated or based on the color of their skin.

And yet we have marches that demand that certain groups be given special treatment and compensation for past grievances. The marches demand free services, free food, jobs without experience, free money without working for it, justice though violence and death are in their wake.

How do you answer crimes committed by those who believe violence is their only way of life? This is where the media and government have failed the American people by showing and enhancing the complaints of those who are aggrieved. By not facing the reality of poverty leads us back to our government that has regulated businesses in an overwhelming manner that few can survive. By enhancing racial problems instead of solving them. By overwhelming our society with taxes, regulations and laws to suit the purposes of our government not the people.

Unless we go back to our old way of living and working, we will become a third world nation influencing no one and uplifting our children into citizens of a once great nation will be a distant dream.

Crying out that everyone is treated poorly because they demand a bigger piece of the pie without working for it will only destroy us all. Demanding to start at the top of the ladder before building the ladder will not ever bring satisfaction, but only sad self-centered disillusionment.

Woe is me will never replace look at me. Your success in this country is what you make of it, not what you can take from it. The answer we hear is not that we hold these truths to be self-evident, but that we are all hyphenated Americans and we must be divided forever. This is a Union and if we want to stay as such, we have to understand together why we stand or fall.

If we stand selfishly for ourselves, we shall see the collapse of our nation soon enough.

Chapter Three

When faiths are one,

    there is no faith but chaos.

Christians appear to be self-destructing. Christ is not enough so a touch of reincarnation and Wicca is needed to boost spiritual needs. Some in the gay community as practicing homosexuals hold to be upstanding Christians and claim that it is a gift from God. We have government officials offering Christian advice, but not taking that advice for themselves as they are caught in extramarital affairs, theft, lying and cheating the public.

There is no doubt there is a veil that covers the eyes of the educated and the ignorant concerning the events of this age. ISIS is a threat that brags they will take over Rome and the Vatican. They swear that they will cut off the head of the Pope. ISIS demands a one world religion that will not tolerate any other faith

Yet, what hope do they bring? 72 virgins? Do those 72 virgins have any say in the matter? Not only is sex waved under the noses of mass murderers, but they are praised for all the abominations against humanity. When one uses fear and death to convert, what incentive is there to follow that faith?

The thousands that come to the United States will have members of ISIS that will attack and kill those who live in this country. Why is there so much anger against Christians? We offer Jesus the Christ which is a free offering and we do not have to demand conversion. Judgment is of God not ourselves. We give the message and pray for results. ISIS and their counterparts demand conversion and kill if rejected.

Our government turns its head concerning the beheading and crucifixions of many Christians while propping up the myth that ISIS is only a second class terrorist organization. When will the U.S. wake up? Scripturally, never. Revelation teaches us that no great nation from the west will participate in Armageddon. Our demise is certain, but we are aiding that demise by allowing all kinds of perversion and crime to be acceptable under the constitutional and spiritual law. We deny God, we shake our fist at the Cross, we laugh at the written Resurrection and think God will laugh with us.

    No wonder there are problems with many who question Christianity. If no one seeks to read or understand God's Word, if Christ is not real enough to ease the fear of death, if life is less exciting by leading a godly life, then it all makes perfect sense. Believe only what makes you comfortable, what makes you acceptable to society, whatever leads you down the road never to be taken. If God is less in your eyes than yourself, then be free, be happy, eat, drink and be merry for when the darkness comes and you find out the truth you can always blame the darn Republicans. All the liberals do.

Chapter Four

Statements of Belief

I believe if you don't vote, you voted for the one you didn't want to win.

I believe if you accept all a candidate tells you that you are more of a blithering idiot than are.

I believe if you think terrorism is not as bad as they say it is, then one day you will be a victim and wonder what happened.

I believe offering love when someone holds a gun or knife to your head is as foolish as jumping out of a plane without a parachute.

I believe if you think socialism is the wave of the future, then wait for that wave bury you in poverty, subjugation, dictatorship and disease.

I believe if you don't believe in God what you will say when you meet Him?

I believe if you think all refugees are law abiding future citizens, I hope they live next to you.

I believe if you vote for the wrong candidate no matter who they represent, you will always blame the Republicans.

I believe if you think the Bible is archaic nonsense, maybe we should start building another Ark or invest in fireproof suits.

I believe if life, liberty and the pursuit of happiness only means your life, your liberty and pursuit of your pleasure; you will lose that life, liberty and all happiness for the pleasure of the government.

I believe if someone slaps you it is alright to slap

them back except for lawyers and police unless political correctness or federal law telling you not to.

I believe in the right to life, that an unborn baby has a soul, a right to breathe the same air and a chance to succeed or fail in their own right. Also, despite the wishes of arrogant men and women claiming Whoopsie! My bad!

I believe in a hostile world and yet there can be peace.

I believe you cannot negotiate peace with an ideological horror that believes no one should live unless catering to a moon god.

I believe in a living God not a symbol, a rock or a physically formed entity that refuses to talk back.

I believe that sexual deviation brings disease, heartbreak, confusion of identity, anger, atheism, prejudice and shame.

I believe terrorism can only be stopped by violence not negotiations and prayer.

I believe having temper tantrums in Congress is a childish act for not getting their way. If Republicans did it, it would still be a childish act.

I believe that our country is dumbing down its citizens with electric toys and vacuous movies.

I believe without God, children will continue to kill children, husbands will kill wives and family, and mass slaughter will continue for an imaginary Valhalla.

I believe public education leads to third grade level graduates rather than fourth grade college graduates.

I believe not teaching real history, history will certainly repeat itself.

I believe there are no hyphenated Americans only hyphenated prejudice that denigrates freedom.

I believe the Constitution should not be torn

apart by the Supreme Court because they are looking for what the meaning of is, is.

I believe Democrats should not ignore criminal acts because the ones involved weren't Republicans.

I believe neither Republican of Democrat is perfect.

I believe if you are a royal pain in the neck, you should see a Chiropractor.

I believe if you think Sharia Law should be invoked, maybe you should you find some other country that accepts it.

I believe we should bring back the Wonderful World of Disney. The world could use an hour of fantasy bliss.

I believe in the last days, Armageddon and the Rapture.

I believe most people do not understand the Rapture or the narrow road to Heaven

I believe because you think all people go to Heaven because they are famous or good should try and be famous and good themselves without Christ. See how it works out for you.

I believe in death and Resurrection, but Resurrection for those who believe in Christ and His statement "I am the Way, the Truth and the Life, no one comes to the Father but through Me."

I believe in fresh baked bread, cookies, pudding and ice cream.

I believe the same things bring high cholesterol, fat and heart disease.

I believe without difficult experiences you have delicate egos that prance around within political correctness.

I believe criminals convicted or not should be suspect for higher office.

I believe marriage is a lifelong experience in love.

I believe in God and no other.

I believe in Christ and no other.

I believe I have run out of things to believe in, how about you?

Chapter Five

The deflation of America?
Why? What for?

What great wonders are left in this world if the destructive force of lies takes the wonder out of our awe concerning the greatness of our country, our faith and our own lives? The awe of our country is that we are still the freest people in the world. We still have the opportunity to further our dreams despite government interference, the awe of our faith that God can still answer prayer despite the ACLU and the liberal press, the awe of our own lives despite the ravages of abortion, euthanasia and forced poverty. We can still work for financial security. We can still seek eternal life and we can keep ourselves healthy even with the onslaught of disease and Obama Care.

Our country is unique and under a constant barrage of jealousy, hate and attack when many want to undo the last avenue to Eden in this world. Why not emulate our freedom? Because God still abides with us we thrive through God's good grace and if we allow to be conquered from within, our enemies win. So why is selfishness easier to accept than selflessness? When is fifteen minutes of fame more important than a lifetime of service, devotion and hard work?

We are turning into a cancerous nation feeding on each other as fame junkies and ego cannibals. If we continue to feed off those who succeed because we are too weak to succeed on our own, we not only defeat ourselves, but commit societal suicide. It's always easier to be a coward then stand and fight for your country, your family or your God. The spirit of our past is fast evaporating within this fog of self-absorption. Since when did we insist on becoming a third world nation when we were Camelot where everyone wanted to come to live? We were not lucky, we were blessed. Now we live with self-hatred and envy. Who told us to believe such nonsense? Only your silence has made it so.

You must know that life is like a puppy dog. Sometimes he wets the floor and other times craps in your lap. Either way you have to clean up the mess. It's a crude analogy, but nothing seems to go right at times and we have to correct the problems we set up for ourselves.

What is it that a country like ours would have so many people dissatisfied with freedom, God and a chance to succeed? When has anarchy and selfishness taken over law and order? Having become so self-centered that those who live in poverty and a religious vacuum are insignificant because they don't meet our needs as a society? Our churches avoid spiritual fulfillment for crowded pews with deep pockets and a need to avoid meaningful scripture.

    We don't wish to offend which our faith in Christ will certainly do if it does not condone gay marriage, all roads lead to heaven, abortion and political correctness. What is the threat of Christianity that brings about the martyrdom of thousands by the sword of ISIS? What is the purpose of Christianity if we whisper the Word of God hoping no one will hear us? Why does God still walk with us when the world is going up in flames? Do we think that no matter what we do God will forgive us without asking for it? The confusion of faith is that we spend too much time making excuses for our sins instead of asking for forgiveness for those same sins? Do we argue with God and say "Excuse me, God, I have a better idea." God's only answer would be "Really?"

It is not wrong to fear death. We all worry about the unknown and no one wants to be rejected. However, our society demands to be accepted no matter the crime, no matter the sin. Two things will happen which is absolute. The first is that nothing erases memory of the truth. The second is we stand before God for good or ill. I would think the fear of God's judgment would be enough to temper our lives toward some good at least. The nihilistic view of life can never satisfy, just destroy happiness.

Standing before God is too late to say to Him "If I only knew." Or "Why didn't you tell me plainly?" God will say "I sent many messengers to you and My Word was there for you to read. You have no excuse and this is My house not yours." And it is true that there is an innate feeling in all of us that there is something more to our lives. We just choose selfishness and greed to circumvent sacrifice and charity. Too many believe success and wealth means God's blessings on us. How do we determine God's blessing on those who are beheaded and crucified by terrorists?

    We in America are too complacent in our spiritual lives. We are not challenged enough. How would you react if threatened? What if your boss tells you not to talk about your faith? Do you become silent? If a terrorist puts a gun to your head and threatens to shoot you unless you deny Christ, do you deny or defy? How do you live your life if you make excuses for your sins? How do we allow others at work to abuse you, steal from you and gossip about you to see if your faith is true? How do you forgive?

    We have come at a crossroads in our country where we will deny our Christian heritage, demand God accept our ways instead of His ways down a path to socialism and atheistic corruption. These things exclude freedom to worship, freedom to speak, freedom to pursue happiness.

    We quiver in corners to speak against the tyranny that is coming. We shiver at the thought of dictatorship, but the silence is deafening. Our children ignore the signs as the spirit of life expires right before our eyes. We do not worship at the altar of Heaven, but government which only leads to slavery, chains of poverty and the void of God. No other hell could be worse.

We are Americans who fought against tyranny. We stand by the Constitution or do we? We believe in freedom, but freedom is costly with a price that has to be paid. We believe in God though the elite tell us it is not so. Should we give up? If we do, we become a third world nation that deserves its fate and it will be our own fault.

Are we to be a police state or submit to anarchy? Do we have to bleed again in and through civil war because we lost sight of the wonderful life we could share? Do we hate ourselves that much we should destroy the most unique country in the world? Do nations hate us because they are jealous and lack the will to be free?

We are not here for handouts. We did not toil and fight for our liberty to allow it to be stolen from us by those who think they can get something for nothing. By those who think subjugation and tyranny is the new world order. Where has our heritage gone? Has it been an alcoholic vision of frustration and weariness enhanced by medical and mind numbing drugs?

Will it be to abandon our God thinking we can do all things on our own? Look at the failures around you who we call leaders. Look at the greed of those who run businesses who throw away employees as fast as they employ them. Look at those who think they have no value listening to false claims of lotteries and government subsidies. Some say socialism is the answer, but where has it worked that communism and tyranny have not taken its place? If this is your belief then you have nothing in this life or the next.

Be assured there is a judgment whether it be dust to dust or standing before God realizing what you accepted was a false truth for the real truth that judges you. What is your purpose if you have no purpose? Where comes the peace? The understanding? The faith? When the darkness comes who shall bring the light? Why insist there is something where nothing exists?

Chapter Six

Ah, Let's Just Go For It.

    Where is the consciousness of America? There is no thought to abortion. There is no thought to gay marriage. There is no thought to Christianity other than to ignore it all for the sake of political correctness. The backbone of America seems arthritic, financially bankrupt and politically confused. We will cry out loud for the head of a man who killed a lion, but not a whisper for the millions who died from a doctor's knife. Who cries out for the unborn?

    When do we stop being cowards with our heads in the ground because we do not want to confront Iran, ISIS, Russia or any other group that wants to destroy our nation? We are still a godly nation, but for some reason we think that is a sign of weakness. We are still considered the Great Satan and we feel the need for political correctness to not change that image. We seek to apologize when no apology is needed.

Many in our society want to eradicate all vestiges of Christianity to keep peace with those aggressive people who are offended by our faith. It doesn't matter the excuses, the wrongful historical myths, the slavery or the claims of faithless politics we are a unique nation under God. If we decide to hide the Cross like Obama did at Georgetown University so as not to offend, we deny the faith that has no option but to offend those who do not believe.

No one wants to acknowledge the fulfillment of scripture that is happening before our eyes. Our arrogance to save life (abortion), to stay healthy (introducing drugs and free marijuana) or keep us free (government handouts and food stamps) will not save us. We were founded upon Judeo-Christian principles that give all men freedom and the ability to work for self-sufficiency. It is incredible that having put ourselves under government bondage we still think we are free.

Now the new world order is coming starting with the influx of Middle East refugees into Europe to dilute their culture and government where these refugees though needing to escape will never give up their faith and eventually demand Sharia Law. The United States will not be immune as Obama and Kerry will now allow hundreds of thousands who do not want anything, but to be free to do as they please in a society that is governed by law, democratic law founded by men who had no thoughts for giving it up for Sharia Law.

And what percentage of these refugees are infiltrating our borders with intent to cause havoc and death to those who are innocent? ISIS has already said some of those who come to our shores are part of their group because there will be little vetting of those who we allow in. There is no protest for anyone who comes to our shores, but it is imperative that they speak English, accept our culture and laws. It is expected from our countries immigrants that anyone who comes to them accept the language, culture and laws of their lands. This is not bigotry, but common sense for if we allow the culture and laws to be corrupted, we will no longer be America, the land of the free.

Violence is growing because there is no respect of the law, but chaos and mobs are trying to rule the outcome of crimes instead of the courts. Even then, if these mobs do not like the outcome they will destroy their own neighborhoods in protest. What madness is this? I will tell you. When faith in God is taken out of the schools and colleges, the churches deal in apologetics instead of scripture, the government circumvents the bill of rights and the media mocks God there is nothing left to believe in.

We have already seen the wide road and the

narrow road deciding to take the one filled with travelers rather than the one to travel alone or by the few. It is easy to follow the crowds thinking we are less responsible for our actions, but we will all, believer or not, will stand before God in judgment. I already hear the derision and mock laughter for writing that statement. As archaic as you may think it is, it is the one constant for our future.

If one delves into scripture and prophesy, you can see the events of this age are becoming clear and sure. In the end good will fight evil. Already the Koran is very clear that anyone other than the follower of Mohammed must be converted or killed. Who has not heard of the thousands of Christians being beheaded, children raped, women defiled and those who will not yield being crucified. Who cries out for them? Our country is silent when it comes to our government and the news. Who says it will not come here if we continue to sleep through the horror?

We hear constant complaints about how horrible

our country has been. Violent marches display the anger of various groups who do not have the answer and how to make a change for the better. Well, where would you rather be? Iran? Iraq? Any European nation that has embraced socialism and is suffering economically? Hey, how about Venezuela with 700% inflation, high unemployment, Caracas the murder capital of the world or Mexico where drug cartels rule?

Could you protest there as freely as here in the United States? Where is free speech more prevalent than here? Tell me this is not a country blessed by God where we have not suffered the destruction that is now going on in the world? We are a group of individuals where individuality may be sacred, but it is not the end all of a nation.

If you want special attention, then work for it and don't become a special group wanting dispensation and free money because you feel different. No apologies because you don't get the attention you think you deserve.

Crybabies seem to rule the day because they can't have Sharia Law, are mad to learn the English language, know the Constitution and obey the laws of the land. We see their fists shake at our faith and cries we will not obey. Every country demands you learn the language, integrate with their society and obey their laws.

We are losing our heritage because insane policies use political correctness as a means not to offend causes of transgender, gay marriage, atheistic programs, abortion and Christian intolerance.

We can tolerate any group except those that wish to change our society into a mess of immorality masquerading as normal. Their belief is that no one should be excluded in our society as long as immorality be demanded to be blessed by God. Should our laws be absconded by perverted influences just so we don't offend?   A prime example is the demand from the gay community that churches, against scriptural law, to be blessed in marriage or share the pulpit. Why? If civil ceremonies are allowed must the church be forced to succumb to these demands? The gay agenda wants special privileges over and above ordinary citizens. When one demand is met a second, a third will be demanded. The same will be said about the transgender issue. The use of bathrooms are only the beginning. The moral values of a few should not be forced on everyone else.

Are we intolerant? Yes, we are. Just as intolerant as Muslims who demand we forsake all for Allah or die! Christians do not threaten death if Muslims don't convert. Where are the peaceful intentions?

Arrogance that has no respect for life while thumbing your nose at God will have its consequences. Many scoff because the use of God and Bible, not to mention the name of Jesus, is deemed archaic though Allah is not. Since when is trying to save children archaic? Since when is trying to keep individuals from moral decay and disease archaic? When has the Bible become politically incorrect?

When have the Constitution, moral respect, freedom of speech and press become reprehensible to the society who wants to know the truth? What is the truth? God was the basis of founding this country and when we turn our backs on Him, He will do the same. Chaos and destruction follows as we are seeing in the Middle East.

Christianity has found a wall of intolerance and some have replaced it with tolerance of selective reasoning. Should we substitute a moon god for the living spiritual One? One a rock and a star, the other an empty grave and a Cross? Christianity teaches a moral absolute though it is difficult to be moral absolutely.

Our country is under attack with such things as the National Anthem being a display of racism! The church is exclusive to everyone who will not abide to its tenants. That part is true since following Christ is essential or why bother to go to any church?

If you feel this country is not for you, look to

other countries and find any one that will fulfill your demands. Where else can anyone live peacefully in their faith, have a chance to become successful or even become famous without being a criminal? We can listen to fools that think Socialism is the answer or the key to success. What country allows the same chances for success than here?

9/11 proved we were so successful that jealous enemies tried to kill that image. We are the Great Satan because we are free and successful. Other nations are mostly rubble, live in poverty, hope their children don't die of starvation or disease and suffer under dictatorships. We are considered a Christian nation which puts a target on our backs. Other nations called it arrogance, but we call it confidence. Why else do so many people try to come to our shores? If we were the Great Satan why do immigrants come and stay here?

Chapter Seven

Politics or Not?

Should we be a Conservative or Liberal Socialist country? There doesn't seem to a middle ground. Conservatives do not accept abortion rights because the rights of the unborn are ignored. The Liberal mind believes that all women have the right to destroy fetuses especially if they interfere with their lifestyle. Few abortions are to save the life of the mother. It's mostly inconvenience.

Conservatives do not want to be forced to accept gay weddings if they are forcing the church to sanction the union. Most conservatives would allow civil ceremonies, but the church should be allowed as a matter of scripture to refuse to bless such a union. Liberals demand that God be ignored and the church accept homosexuality as normal. The big question is why it is so important the church acknowledge something against its faith?

Conservatives want lower taxes so that they can keep more of the money they earn. Liberals want more taxes to give to those who refuse to work or are unable to work so they will be responsible voters for the Democratic Party. Liberals want free medical, but want those who work to foot the bill. Liberals want more money to give to illegal aliens, pet projects and gain power over taxpayers.

Conservatives want to slow national debt by less spending and a smaller government. Liberals want to pay off debt by higher taxes on the rich which they can't agree the bottom line of who to tax. The interesting thing is that if you took all money of the rich, you would get about $100 billion toward the national debt. This would leave only $20.9 Trillion left to pay. Where does the rest of the money come from? Liberals will say to not take it from us!

Regulations and higher corporate taxes will not ease the national debt, however raising corporate taxes will mean fewer employees and less taxes with more inflation to pay those taxes. New Jersey tried to do this and the companies fled the state. If you do it nationwide, then companies will leave the country. How is this a win-win situation?

Now I'm confused why a 38% tax rate on businesses will help expand corporations to hire more people. How does raiding corporate profits encourage helping the economy? Does anyone in Congress know simple math and basic economics? Why do you think corporate headquarters are moving overseas? Could it be they pay half in taxes of what they earn? Wouldn't you like to keep more of what you earn? Doesn't 12% sound better than 38% for corporations? Doesn't 10%-12% sound better to live the American dream for taxpayers?

It is also seen that medical corporations raise their fees to exorbitant prices to make sure whatever the government decides to fine them can be paid as well as make crazy profits. Don't we all want to hedge our bets against what our government may want to take from us?

Conservatives believe that God is alive while Liberals believe God should mind His own business. Conservatives believe the church should have a say in government as when we first formed our nation. Liberals think the Bible is irrelevant, the church needs separation from the state, and does not fulfill the needs of society and death is final. Now the church is infiltrated with political correctness more than scripture.

Disillusioned voters refuse to vote because they see corruption. Conservatives will probably refuse to vote and we will have another extension of the failed

Obama administration, another $10 Trillion in debt in 8 years, less religious liberty, medical inflation and higher taxes. Liberals don't care about inflation, debt or religious liberty. It interferes with the imprisonment of a society that is free and can make its own future.

We are on the verge of a socialist state and Liberals don't care. Socialism leads to tyranny which in turn control the banks, assets of the retired, higher taxes and national bankruptcy. Look at Greece, Venezuela and various other countries. We would see high inflation like Venezuela which was 200% this past year and now reached 700% with scarcity of food and essential products. I repeat this information for those who little understand the danger.

The population is exploding with anger and hate. The motto Black Lives Matter, but no one else matters. Illegal aliens matter, but not our citizens. The gay movement is undermining moral integrity and defile the church. These movements are only to divide this country to collapse the freest nation in the world.

When God is taken out of our society there is no hope for the family, the community, the government or our schools. It is why we see such an uptick in crime and murder.

Speaking of violence, now the government is challenging the Second Amendment that no one should have a gun. They claim it is to keep guns out of the hands of terrorists and criminals. Really? Weapons are flowing over our southern border without detection and sold on the black market. They defy the law, so who is going to get hurt by banning guns? More liberal insanity.

Now the real crazy part. Liberals want to ban guns yet they are allocating the following budgets to purchase firearms for government officials:

$11.7 million to Dept. of Veterans Affairs.

$10.7 million for I.R.S. (better pay your taxes or else)

$4.8 million Animal and Plant Inspection Services.

What? You're going to arm animals and plants? Does that include bullet proof vests?

$2.8 million Bureau of the Public Debt. Pay your debts or the it's firing squad for you.

$1.02 million for National Oceanic and Atmospheric Administration. Something fishy there.

$815,000 Food and Drug Administration. I would seriously keep from the pasta in case of a stray spent bullet.

$417,000 Social Security Administration. Those old people may get rowdy as their checks suddenly stop in the near future.

$413,000 Dept. of Education. That's right we can stop violence in the school by arming the educational leadership.

$309,000 Smithsonian Institution. We can't have the exhibits get out of hand, can we?

$262,000 National Institute of Standards and Technology. The standard must be shot to kill, especially those AI robots going rogue.

$76,000 Small Business Administration. Small business, small allocation.

$44,000 Railroad Retirement Board. Need guns to hold up the railroads to pay for retirement.

Yes, we must keep guns out of the hands of people so we can have a police state. Next, liberals will want to ban knives. Why? On July 26, 2016 in California at a Traditionalist Worker Party rally. Ten people were stabbed and sent to hospitals while others carried sticks. There have been reports of multiple stabbings in Israel, Great Britain, China and Oklahoma. I say Oklahoma because a fertilizer bomb blew apart the Alfred P. Murrah Federal Building in Oklahoma City in April, 1995. Two stabbings at Maumee State Park in Oregon drew national attention.

So do we ban the possessions of knives and fertilizer? Where does it end? So many people are fat and lazy, do we ban forks and spoons as if they are the cause of their largess? The problem is with the minds of those who cannot express themselves any other way or have been taught that violence is the only answer. How is this possible? Try teaching children that there is no God. Try teaching children we just exist from a long ago explosion and there is nothing, but the here and now. Try teaching them that socialism is good thing as long as you don't look at Greece, Venezuela and numerous other countries living in squalor. If you teach ignorance, ignorance will overcome logic, faith and freedom.

Chapter Eight

Kill Me, Kill You
What's the Difference?

Suicide, murder or suicide/murder is overtaking the country. Eight dead in Ohio, six dead in Georgia with no remorse and little reason and we ask why? This happened in 24 hours in April, 2016. Where is the blame for individuals that kill and maim for whatever reason. As this country progresses it sinks deeper into an abyss of atheistic hypocrisy, life becomes meaningless.

How does this happen? Do we take it back when God was left out of the classroom? Do we blame the church for the cultural change? Has political correctness overwhelmed our society so much that anything we do is okay? We need to teach that moral teaching and rules of law are important to keep a society from falling apart.

What do we teach in the classroom that circumvents even the laws of nature? What do we teach on Cable T.V. that crime pays? Cheating on your husband or wife is acceptable? That the church is overrated and archaic when it comes to real rules? The law? Moral integrity?

Is there an excuse for everything? Do we accept women are superior and men are thugs? All lives don't really matter? Christians are evil and all other faiths live in peace? Socialism will inherit the earth? Capitalism is the road to poverty? Who believes this stuff? However, this is what we are being taught in all parts of society. Ignorance seems to be the new genius. The facts don't matter as long as we can party all night.

Just recently archeologists claim they found

chariot wheels, bones of horse and men at the bottom of the Red Sea. It was relegated to a future episode for the Discovery station. This is a huge find verifying a historical chapter of the Bible, but the few elite don't want to give anyone hope and further proof that the Bible is true. You cannot demoralize a nation if you give them hope.

Where is the voice of the church? We heard from some churches concerning the Ark built in Kentucky. Instead of support, they complained about the fact that state taxes were being used for the park. They yell about Separation of Church and State when no such thing exists in the Constitution! Go to Russia if you want separation of Church and State.

The madness of the church is that it feels it should not intervene in Government business, yet that was precisely a part of the original United States. If you haven't seen what taking God out of all public view has caused, you live in a vacuum with ignorance and vacant bliss. We didn't win this country by kicking God out of the equation. We cannot rule without faith, moral codes and justice. We succeed because God had His hand on us despite ourselves because we rely on Him looking over our shoulders. Now we say God be damned, we're going to do it our way. How's that working out for you?

Chapter Nine

The Saints come marching in,
but why are they carrying swords?

Will we wait until ISIS comes to us from within before we say "Enough!" How many "refugees" will be brought into our country harboring a per cent of terrorists that have not been vetted by our government? ISIS has said it will send some of their own. We have already had Christians assassinated in Charleston, S.C. and an Oregon college campus. Russia is beginning to fulfill prophecy that has the whole world against Israel. Some leaders of the U.S. have said Israel is on its own.

Does our government really believe we are

safe from terrorism if we just stay out of the Middle East? Does our government believe if we ignore it, keep it out of the public eye that we will be safe from it? The Koran tells all that anyone-ANYONE- who does not believe in Allah (historically a moon god not the God of the bible) should be killed or enslaved. Thousands of Christians have been slaughtered in the Middle East so where is it that we see a peaceful religion?

Some Christians regale the Jews though was not Jesus a Jew? The Muslims speak of Abraham as their father, was not Abraham a Jew? The madness continues.

It has become more certain that we are in the last days. Russia, China, Iran and the rest of the Middle East are convinced that this is the time to take over the world. Sharia Law needs to be invoked if Allah is to bring its own messiah to destroy Jews and Christians from the face of the earth.

We know it will not happen because Christ will

come again to save His people. The evil Jesus Islam talks about is not the answer. The Muslim clerics have relayed the message that the evil Jesus will destroy all those who speak against Allah. We have a government that is blinded by the spirit of Antichrist to allow our destruction by inaction and fear.

There will be more attacks in our country because Political Correctness is cultural insanity. Scripture tells us that certain moral issues must be addressed. The Lord has told us that certain things are a sin and will not be tolerated. Do we ask for forgiveness? No, because we want what satisfies us now whether sexually or monetarily. We will do whatever our Sodom and Gomorrah moment fulfills the lust of the moment. God destroyed Sodom and Gomorrah for its sins and defiance of God. Our country will suffer the same if we ignore the truth.

We in the United States became the greatest nation, despite its flaws, in the world. When we degrade ourselves and defy God in our selfishness, we are doomed. We are becoming self-centered and ignorant to the dangers of our society. No one wants responsibility for our choices whether it's killing millions of babies without regret or accepting socialism as the only way of life.

Why argue the point when speaking to the culturally deaf? Repeating history is easy, making history is not.

Chapter Ten

This is the vision of those
    who say there is no God.

We believe in nothing.
We seek nothing.
Time is meaningless.
All roads lead to death.
We seek the madness
Of the tomb and the grave.
Who dares to care for living?
Living is dust alive
Returning to dust in the wind.
Who looks for life
Will find the path
That leads to other paths

That treads on dust
Which was once alive
Now creeps between the toes
and clogs the nose
While a sneeze will
wipe out every generation.

Chapter Eleven

One thinks the smartest things
at awkward moments
and end in years with no one to listen.

    I have worked with men who have no honor, no decency. They try to terrorize those who work with them. Few kind words just angry threats over the racial divide which has only changed who are the masters. Women demand equal rights then demand to be compensated for the lost years of female financial subjugation. Black lives matter, but no one else's life matters is the new byword. The glass ceiling must be broken. Yes, it can be broken, but by hard work and intelligent thought. You cannot break the glass ceiling unless you have the wherewithal to lead.

Leading does not entail malice, revenge, greed, anger or the persecution that keeps oneself from advancing. You cannot succeed unless the "I" is replaced with the "we". A corporation does not succeed being a socialist entity, but a Capitalist one. You want to sell products to make money not give it all away.

At the writing of this book a presidential hopeful has declared he is a devoted socialist and wants to share the wealth. Why would anyone want to try and succeed if all the work he/she has done is to be given to others who did not share your success? Why would anyone do their best if mediocrity is the goal? In Football, why have the Super Bowl if everyone gets a trophy engraved with "Thanks for coming!" Or have sports events where everyone is paid the same and everyone tries their hardest not to get hurt or stand out with gifts God has given them?

A liberal senator claims that the conservative running for Vice President Mike Pence, who claims to be a Christian, is intolerant and backward thinking. Christians, Republicans, conservatives and those who believe in smaller government with less taxes are demonized by the left.

Christians because they believe right to life, marriage between man and woman and respect for God is no longer the norm for this country. It is considered intolerant to allow people to do whatever they want sexually, morally or financially.

Republicans are demonized because they believe in Capitalism to succeed, not handouts, the right of the individual not the right of government and belief in the Constitution.

Conservatives are demonized because they invoke the right of law to solve problems, not riots with destruction of private property.

Then there are those miscellaneous that want a smaller government that will not add taxes, free rides for anyone who demands it, endless regulations, demilitarizing to the point of making our country less safe and restrictions on guns. The last one, restriction of guns is laughable since many crimes are committed by guns that were sold on the black market. Many more crimes are committed by knives, rocks and wooden sticks.

To get back on point, why is it so hard to see that socialism doesn't give out free gifts? Somebody has to pay for them? Why work if everything is free? Of course another presidential candidate likes giving away free gifts such as health insurance, food stamps and lifelong unemployment insurance good as forever stamps from the Post Office.

Liberalism is not a constitutional right and is not God's plan for this country. From the start we have had a work ethic that has driven this country, led our country to its greatness. Our greatness is not perfect, but has had its share of problems, that of slavery, racial and ethnic prejudice, poverty and political madness.

Yet, this is the country that everyone wants to come to and, also, the one others want to destroy.

Tyranny permeates the rest of the world and those who live under tyranny want to escape it. How many Americans are running to China, North Korea or Russia to better themselves? Where is God and salvation in those countries? Where is Free Speech, Free Press or Freedom of Religion? The last freedom, that of religion is now being tested in this country as Islam is excused for its intolerance and violence while the media criticizes Christianity concerning education, history and the very Constitution that our country is based on.

Almost every state of the union acknowledges in its preamble a higher being, God as a testimony to its right to exist as a state. The very basis of our freedom and existence is attested to by our forefathers which comes from God. The very basis of our greatness has been to acknowledge God and His blessings. Yet we now deny His involvement with our success. How can we wonder about the chaos, acceptance of immorality, the silence of the church and our slow economic collapse unless we look within and without our responsibility?

How many have read the Constitution or the Declaration of Independence? How many believe we are the worst nation to live in? I keep hearing various hyphenated Americans cry about not being head honchos without working for it? Why do we concern ourselves with hyphens anyway?

This is a country that demands excellence from its citizens. And why not? Why would half measures do? If you fail, pick yourself up again and take the opportunity to succeed. If you succeed, turn to the next person and help them achieve their goals. Remember you cannot demand respect. You earn it.

Why do we have to have the Constitution or the Declaration of Independence reinterpreted for us by socialist intellectuals who would rather destroy the law than uphold it. They would rather destroy all moral obligations by denying God a voice in our government. Why has the Constitution been upheld for the first 200 years and now the last 60 is believed to be antiquated by those who think it is not fair to all?

What isn't fair is that our children have not been given the chance to understand our freedoms, our original form of government and the moral backbone that made us great. Now they are taught to use violence, ignore God and demand whatever vice they want to demean themselves whether it hurts someone else or not.

When self-centeredness rules what happens to moral justice, Judeo-Christian values and rule of law? Why is Judeo-Christian values a danger to an upright society? Would you rather Sharia Law? Law of the jungle? Complete Anarchy?

Have we changed freedom of religion to accept all religions to confound and rule our country excluding, of course, Judeo-Christian ethics. Many want to deny the foundation of our nation which is freedoms coming from God not Allah, the Bible not the Koran, moral reason not subjugation, common sense not anarchy. We are at the crossroads between a free nation or a nation of chaos.

Yes, the people rule and our government is closing in on a dictatorship. Yet the way things are, they both lead to the break from the rule of law. Should we reinstate the guillotine? Do we behead the rich that offer jobs to everyone?

The answer to our financial problems lie in lower corporate and individual taxes, less government intrusion and the realization that WE the people can make ourselves equal by not choosing sides, but work to bring back the America that was successful.

Our forefathers did not die for this nation to be suppressed by another King George allowing this nonsense of every man for himself, living in an unreasonable future and selfish egotism.

Bringing up slavery, the Civil War, past corruptions and bigotry will not free ourselves now. We must protect ourselves with the cloak of the Constitution and comfort ourselves in the Bible. Now I've said it where all you liberals will cry out I'm a religious bigot who lives in the past. If the past can save the future of our country, I'm all for it.

When I was a child, I walked the streets without fear. My parents never worried if I would come home or be left in the street to die. I walked miles until I was in high school without the dread of strangers passing me by. Now many die each day walking the streets of our nation.

The real issue is we are shaking our fists at God without regret and expect the best to happen. We distrust God and think we can stand alone. What fool thinks we have been blessed without a purpose?

All the rioting, higher murder rates and massacres now happening is a direct result of our lack of faith. Upticks in rape, divorce, family destruction and anti-government are to be expected when unemployment, spiritual bankruptcy and financial distress overwhelm a country where government and churches ignore the problem. We will collapse under such a burden.

Why do we cry out for justice and mercy when the demand for revenge is so great? Where is the common sense within the bastion of selfishness that relies on the me instead of the we?

Who can tolerate, for the sake of a family or a nation, some of the fool's errands that the media thinks is fair? Fair to whom? Us? Them? Will we be a sinking ship or pull up the sails to come back home? Now the real question is where is home? There are two signposts on the road back. One says God and freedom and the other hell and subjugation.

Hell and subjugation leads to places like Greece, Venezuela, Russia and China. Why would anyone emigrate there? The sign God and freedom leads us here where dreams can come true, faith and hard work brings success.

There are many who have decided that their misery is better for them where they can bury their heads in the sand and scream so no one hears us. No danger they believe will come to them because they won't see it coming. At the last minute, they think God will save and protect them even though they didn't ask for it. Their shelter is built on isolating ignorance with the basement of prejudice to hide themselves in.

We forget how we became independent and shame our forefathers by wanting to bring tyranny, slavery and socialism back into this country. We are free men allowing political insects to change our way of life. We look to enslave ourselves to men who do not care about liberty, but power. Existential politics instead of God. Worse they have no desire for your freedom, but theirs alone.

If you think this country is not good enough for you, find one that is because most of us like what we have. You cannot claim blindness for the worst of this nation because it is not perfect and neither are you.

When the end comes many will say how did we get to this state? Look in the mirror and ask again.

Chapter Twelve

Excuse me God, I have a better idea.
God: Really?

What is it that a country like ours would have so many people dissatisfied with freedom, God and a chance to succeed? When has anarchy and selfishness taken over law and order? Have we become so self-centered that those who live in poverty and a religious vacuum are insignificant because they don't meet our needs?

Our churches avoid spiritual fulfillment for waving hands, mumbling prayer language and dancing in the aisles. Many seek to avoid meaningful scripture.

In the 70's and 80's I visited many churches that

had nebulous non-threatening messages. There are some who fulfill the message of Christ without fanfare. The slow creeping instigation condoning all sin, all roads lead to Heaven, abortion and political correctness will certainly destroy the message of Christ.

Christianity causes consternation to those who do not want to listen and live a Godly life. True Christianity has brought the martyrdom of thousands by ISIS. They died for the reality of Christ and one has to wonder how many in this country would do the same? What is the purpose of one's faith in Christ if we whisper the Word of God hoping no one will hear it outside church walls?

Why does God still walk with us when so many ignore the world in flames? Have we become so comfortable that we think no matter what we do God will forgive us without asking for it? The confusion of faith is that we spend too much time making excuses for our sins instead of seeming to confront them and asking for forgiveness.

Furthermore, it is not wrong to fear death. We all worry about the unknown, but it is known when properly explained in scripture. Two things will happen with one standing before God and the other the void of separation from God. This is absolute and irrevocable that judgment will come. No matter how hard you laugh and thumb your nose at God, He has the last say. The second is that in order to listen to judgment we have our memories, our regret and knowledge of a life. How else will we be grateful or leave in sorrow for that judgment? I've said this before and it is important to understand it.

It is true that there is an innate feeling in all of us that there is something more than this life. If not, what real purpose is there to live than take whatever we can and live vicariously? Why marry if sex is readily available? Why work if you can take whatever you want? If we're going to die anyway without purpose, let's have fun! We can just choose selfishness and greed to circumvent sacrifice and charity.

Too many believe success and wealth means God's blessing on us. How do we determine God's blessing on those who are beheaded, living in poverty or face discrimination? We in America seem complacent in our spiritual lives. We are not challenged enough except to determine early service or late service.

The mystery of life is that we deem it a mystery, pure chance or a mistake. We will fight for the right to disbelieve and then fight against those who do.

If life is by chance, is it not necessary to protect that life? Why are teenagers committing suicide at a higher rate? Is it because this life is all there is and they live in despair? That there is no God? No purpose? Told that whatever they do is useless to the future of the world? Ignored? Unloved? How many reasons does one need to be lost, to take one's life?

When anyone cries out, who comforts them? And with what encouraging words? If there is no faith, can you say "God loves you?" Do you say "Things will get better?" How? Why? If there is nothing to live for who can comfort you?

> "The fool says in his heart, 'There is no God." They are corrupt, their deeds are vile; there is no one who does good. The Lord looks down from heaven on the sons of men to see if there are any who understand, any who seek God. All have turned aside..."
>
> Psalm 14: 1-3

The rise of Christianity is felt throughout the world and feared because it brings hope. Islam brings death and discourages freedom. History shows the difference, but the battle comes from ignorance.

Christianity encourages and promises life in this life and the next. What other faith promises a peaceful eternity not sexual entertainment, not reincarnation into a frog or a gnat. Not oblivion and certainly not fertilizer for plants and trees.

What future can be promised to those who suffer if it is not the end of suffering? How does blood lust fulfill the need for peace? How can hate show love? We live in a world that is confused about sexual morality, the worthiness of marriage, the privilege of saving life not taking it and the reality that God exists no matter how many deny him.

Even atheists as they come to the end of their world believe there must be something else beyond death. The young do not fear death until youth fades and the darkness comes upon them.

> "Why do the nations say: 'Where is their God?' Our God is in heaven; he does whatever pleases him. But their idols are silver and gold, made by the hands of men. They have mouths, but cannot speak, eyes, but they cannot see; they have ears, but cannot hear. Noses, but they

cannot smell...those who make them will be like them and so will all who trust in them."

    Psalm 115: 2-8

Chapter Thirteen

Where's The Proof?

Pick a leaf. Pick a rose. Is it by accident? Big Bang Theory? Try a little bang. Empty your shed and put a stick of dynamite inside, light it and wait for the explosion. After the explosion see if there's a small paradise of flowers and trees. Look inside the wreckage and see if there is a Garden of Eden. Maybe a small rodent or even a nest of bees will evolve from the smoke. Explosions destroy things not create for only God can create. The intricate world of Botany and Biology isn't by chance. Evolution teaches by chance and a belief theory without proof. Darwin had his doubts, but avoiding God will never make evolution true.

Now back to the leaf and rose. How did the rose

evolve? A tree? A weed? A rabbit? Evolution cannot be proved, but conjectures like Piltdown Man is not proof. So-called facts deal with a tooth, a rib or a jawbone. So far nothing tangible, but theories looking for the missing link. Theories based on theories based on conjecture.

Evolution is guided by those who want to believe God is non-existent. To what end? To find the fact we are truly finite creatures with no hope except in dust and oblivion? Where is the hope? The Bible has been shown to be a historical and prophesized true collaboration between man and God. Why destroy faith in God if there is nothing better to replace God with? It is only arrogance and irresponsibility to think there is no God, no angelic heaven, just oblivion without thought or existence.

> "The fool says in his heart, 'There is no God.' They are corrupt, their deeds are vile, there is no one who does good. The Lord looks down from

heaven on the sons of men to see if there are any who understand, any who seek God."

Psalm 14: 1,2

The basic tenets of nature prove the existence of God. Natural Law is not happenstance where just by accident there are rules and regulations how all life works. Is it done without thought, meaning or purpose?

What purpose does it serve to believe in the frail nature of man when it is defective in morals and intellect when it comes to making decisions for all of humanity. Moral codes are subjective to the whim of those who rule instead of the moral code of God Himself. Man has always had moments in history to be gods themselves.

> "Come, let us build ourselves a city,
>   with a tower that reaches to the heavens,
> so that we may make a name for

ourselves and not be scattered over the face of the whole earth."

Gen. 11:4

This was the first episode of many who wanted to defy God. Throughout history there have been many rulers and individuals who wanted to be divine. Roman emperors announced their divinity, rulers of Egypt, Hirohito, Dalai Lamas, Kings of Nepal as reincarnations of Vishnu, Narim-Sin, Simon Magus and lists of hundreds throughout history. All these are dead and gone. The only one that claimed to be God was Jesus and He proved it by rising from the dead. None of the others could make that claim.

"Why are you troubled, and why do doubts rise in your minds? Look at my hands and feet. It is I myself! Touch me and see; a ghost does not have flesh and bones as you see I have."

Luke 24: 38,39

Chapter Fourteen

And Now Something Completely Indifferent

In 2015 bones were found in South Africa supposedly being a pre-human. Pre-human? Supposedly the bones are 2.5 – 3 million years old. Can someone tell me how pre-human or not the evidence is acceptable? Known history is 6,000 years old so why haven't we heard historically beyond that time? Can you explain how these pre-humans suddenly became humans able to write, speak and build? Aliens? If aliens, how did they evolve? There had to be a beginning. How did intelligence suddenly appear?

Where is the slow education? Who taught who? Just think rationally about the Big Bang Theory and wonder what started the explosion that haphazardly made semi-perfection nature. How did the earth evolve into a unified machine that heals itself? The basic functions of a human being are not by chance, but by a divine being we call God.

The reason God is not acceptable is because human beings don't want to rely on any Spiritual Being, but will readily accept one when they are on their death bed. It is fascinating that we accept Darwin's Theory, but not the alternative. Even Darwin turned to God in the last days of his life.

We spend so much time denying God rather than seeking him.

> "They claim to know God, but by their actions they deny him."
>
> Titus 1:16

No one likes the idea of someone looking over their shoulder, but if you are doing the right thing, it should not be a problem. It comes from guilt that cheating on your wife causes anxiety. It comes from guilt that even stealing a pen or paper clip gives you pause. You know innately what is wrong or right to do. Who gave you that mental anguish that you wave away as a momentary fit of madness?

> "My guilt has overwhelmed me like a burden too heavy to bear. My wounds fester and are loathsome because of my sinful folly."
>
> Psalm 38: 4,5

It is from experience and visions of past regrets that haunt most individuals. The road not taken, the woman left behind or the job you gave up. My own experience was turning down an art scholarship to go to Nyack Missionary College because of a girl. Bad choice I thought, but that choice led me down a path to my wife.

    I had a variety of jobs which I did mostly well with, but became bored looking for something different. I ended up in retail which ended up being my mission field. If I followed the path to art school would I have been the artist my art teacher in High School, Mr. Dawson, believed me to be? Would I have found the Lord or left Him behind? Everything happens for a reason which leads to the place the Lord sends you. With me, he had a few roadblocks and a wide ditch to move me on the right path.

    "Commit to the Lord whatever you do and your plans will succeed. The Lord works out everything for His own ends."

                  Proverbs 16: 3,4

Each person has a path to take that will lead the right way. It is our pride, our jealousy or lack of faith that will prevent us to live the life we were born to do.

Our school systems took out prayer, U. S. History because it invoked Nationalism and Christian pride. Those who came to this country were Christians, those who fought for the rights we have now were Christians and each state of the union praises God in their individual constitutions.

We are a fallible nation, yet a free nation. Many injustices have been done in the name of God which only meant their faith was corrupted. Our children are paying the price for this lack of faith and we will suffer greatly at their hands if they turn from God.

> "Dear friend, do not imitate what is evil but what is good. Anyone who does what is good is from God. Anyone who does what is evil has not seen God."
>
> John 3: 11

Chapter Fifteen

Are You Paying Attention?

As you may or may have not have noticed, some of the chapters almost repeat themselves. A national survey has found many things have to be repeated before it is remembered. Usually it has to be at least three times. So I say again if you have realized by this point the familiarity of those chapters you have more common sense than most.

So far those who still don't realize the similarities, the following are short sayings and adages that most people will understand. They will be known for their brevity. This is not to say that any of you are ignorant but are discerning in your valuable time for some understanding the limited space that occupies your thoughts.

      Maybe the following bits of knowledge would be more appealing to you.

    Why do you have windows to the soul
when you keep the shades down?

    Who seeks inner peace when
the rest of the world is at war?

    I am worth nothing
if I know nothing.

    All things living
will soon be dead.

    Walking in the path of darkness
is only because you refuse
to turn on the Light.

Who seeks the Lord
and finds Him says:
Who are You?

What does one think of
when growing up?
It is only ourselves.

Till they are fifteen
when it is only girls,

Who seeks the Kingdom of Heaven
when the journey you seek
leads to vacant rooms?

It's frustrating in life
when you open the wrong door
to find another door.

Arrogance is when the Lord says "Follow Me"
when He turns right, you turn left.

God has infinite wisdom
while we have finite wisdom.

Those who think animals are better than humans
have never been scratched or bitten.

Who speaks ill of the dead
unless you're the one who is dead?

How many Socialists are millionaires?
How many Capitalists are billionaires?
Which one is better off?

Who seeks the Kingdom of God
wandering through a sewer?
Ones that bring mops and brooms
to clean them out.

If it's only the echoes of your mind
maybe it's because of empty thoughts
and thoughtless images.

Eternal life is only a bended knee away.

It takes a leap of faith
to get to the other side of Heaven.

The Lord is our Shepherd,
but we don't have to be sleeping sheep.

Socialism is not a competitive sport.

Communism has nothing to do with communes.

Chapter Sixteen

Can We Have An Amen?
Today Not Tomorrow.

Who hears the cries of the children in this country? What kind of education are they getting that means anything except division and diversion? How many times will they be told that there is only this life and no other? Where is the hope? The freedom? The joy of life?

Doubts and fears lurk in the darkness of time. The morning sun wipes away the tears left behind. Is death an eternal oblivious sleep? If so, we won't know it, but if our souls encounter Heaven, tears will come for the wasted years. If we did acknowledge His presence or coming we would surely have lived differently. All things end, others begin if we know for sure the future.

> "Everyone who listens to the Father and learns from him comes to me. No one has seen the Father except the one who is from God, only he has seen the Father. I tell you the truth, he who believes has everlasting life."
>
> John 6: 45-47

Is this myth or legend? Or is it hope and truth? Do we deny and shake with fear the unknown and the inevitable oblivion of death? Or do we trust the Lord and await His coming?

If America is going to fail, it will be by our own will. We beg for a free ride without caring who pays for it. We say we hate individualism, Christianity and the wealthy, but we want success, the death of poverty.

Do you see the obvious inconsistency? We want success by sitting on a soft couch. We expect our enemies to leave us alone if we ignore their aggressions.

We say there is no God except one that must be manufactured from our own minds. There is evidence all around us that we were created not as a small happenstance. We are taught we are own masters, but what has it brought us except poverty, a grave, dust and despondency? Is this America? Where would we go if we continue on this path?

We corrupt history in our schools and expound racism, crime and gender confusion. When did we lose our way? Why do we shake our fist at God when He comes to embrace us? America is not perfect, but we used to strive for the best. Now we show the worst and expect things to get better.

At this writing police officers are being ambushed, black faces are on nightly when crimes are committed and corrupt politicians are being rewarded. These bring forward racism, anarchy and frustration.

Maybe we should legalize abomination and anarchy so that those who want lawlessness and immorality can have their way. Let's ban God and export Christians to have America shaped like other nations who are destroying themselves in the Middle East.

A small, but growing minority have decided that God, Christ and moral behavior is non-essential to the future of our country. The church must take the responsibility to speak against this developing moral abyss through scripture and the voice of God. Oh, wait, I forgot, the church has already accepted parts of the abortion issue, accepted practicing gay ministers in the pulpit and have no say in politics.

We must hold our leaders responsible to represent the majority of this nation, our Constitution and the God that we pledged to honor. Is this happening? No! We have accepted corruption and immorality as a way of life and are afraid to speak against it. Are there consequences? Yes! Is it our moral duty to speak out? Yes! If we don't our faith is dust. Thousands are dying at ISIS hands for their faith. Why are we afraid to demand the best of our leaders?

    Our leaders fear the vocal few who hold the free enterprise system and the church hostage allowing depression, subjugation, poverty and faithlessness to corrupt the greatness that is America. Instead of clucking our tongues we need to stand our ground, voice our opinion, call our congressmen and pray to God for intervention.

    We are close to losing our nation and we cannot elect tyrants to rule our lives. We are the rulers of our own destiny. The government is our servant not our overlord. Teach our children that they have the power to bring us from the brink of disaster, not government. The government is by the people, for the people and of the people not by the Government, for the government and of the government. Leave that to Russia.

Liberals seem to think that any protest against their proposals is founded in hate. Yet when liberals protest, they consider themselves concerned progressive citizens. By progressive I mean another name for socialist.

They offer our children a society without God, free stuff and complacency. When they do this our children will be sacrifice for their luxury not theirs. They offer up Afro-Americans as their new Cause Celebre of the time with a little gender confusion on the side. Liberals get their way through racial division, not inclusion.

Explain to me without the proper education how any problem can be solved without self-reliance? The programs being offered by liberals and the State encourage laziness, high unemployment, crime and no need for an education. We have become a society looking for handouts.

Give me money or give me death! Was that the cry of Patrick Henry? Give me health care or give me rioting in the streets! Give me a job though I am unqualified for it! It's not fair that I am poor and my neighbor is rich! It doesn't matter that he/she worked for it, I want it! I am making $20,000 a year and you are making $200,000. You should give me enough so that we are on an equal financial plain. It's only fair. If it were the other way around it wouldn't be fair because I want to keep my $200,000.

We want socialism, but call it progressive. We want government to control our lives so we can be lazy and arrogant. Let someone else work for us. Let someone else feed us. Let someone else clothe us. Let someone else house us. For this is fair and just in the liberal mindset. Heaven forbid we rely on ourselves and God. We would rather succeed in failure for failure is the new success.

We turn to the government instead of God for our needs. Liberals call themselves progressive to mask their intentions of cultural slavery. We are a free nation because of self-reliance, belief in God,

Capitalism (now a dirty word) and a Constitutional based Government.

It is not perfect, but it is better than any other country in the world or why do so many try to come here? A progressive message is regressive to those things we hold dear and destroys self-esteem, finds success intolerable except for the elite and financial control over everyone.

Is freedom the enemy? Is Capitalism evil? Are Christians the real devil? Is our Republic doomed? Is true education deemed to be dumb-down preaching so young minds can be molded against the precepts of our once proud nation? Should we allow globalism to tear down our borders and imprison ourselves with the hypocrisy of other nations? Should we combine all religions only to destroy every religion? Has God no meaning? Has life no meaning?

Is this far-fetched? Terry McAuliffe. At this year's Democratic convention that now Hillary will bring "forward our government to building a global economy." Another step to a one world government. Do we teach our children in schools and colleges the danger of such a deal? No, they think Bernie Sander's socialist agenda is the right path. They have no idea of the consequences.   Is this madness or God's plan for our unfaithfulness?

> "The righteousness of the upright delivers them, but the unfaithful are trapped by evil desires."
>
> Proverbs 11: 6
>
> "With his mouth the godless destroys his neighbor, but through knowledge the righteous escape."
>
> Proverbs 11: 9
>
> "Through the blessing of the upright a city is exalted, but by the mouth of the wicked it is destroyed."
>
> Proverbs 11: 11

Needless to add anymore if you get my meaning. If we do not listen to God we will in turn go the way of great countries who thought they could survive without Him.

Chapter Seventeen

Christianity Is Not For Cowards

How many Christian men, women and children have been sacrificed because they followed Christ? Now Christians are a danger to society. It must be all that good cheer, love for one another and everlasting life through Christ that disrupts our culture. Or is it because we wish to keep our Republic a democracy, want lower taxes, less government and continued freedom of speech and religion? Or is it because we believe that God has a hand in our country's future?

Is the danger because socialism cannot advance in a Christian society or that our schools might teach moral absolutes or unrevised American History? Never has socialism worked in a free society because socialism silences free speech and steals the ink from freedom of the press.

How do we justify our blessings if God is constitutionally irrelevant? Who plays God when the spiritual void encompasses a nation? These are issues we are going to face in coming elections for our children are taught that faith is irrelevant, sexual activity and deviation is correct, American History is a lie and our biological history comes from an accidental explosion of primal slime.

Where is the hope and salvation of mankind in such thinking? Should we worship blobs of mud and how it is easy to mold an image?

When it comes to prayer, the Lord knows what you are thinking as you pray. Many suffer from the following missteps as they pray one way and think another. This is what the Lord hears:

As you pray, you dream of adultery.

As you pray, you show anger against another.
As you pray, you think of sinful things.
As you pray, you yearn to win the lottery.
As you pray, you become deaf to my voice.
As you pray, you speak only of you.
As you pray, do you listen to My voice?

You ask: "What shall we do then?"

God says: "Learn first that I am your God."

The Lord says that He is not a horn of plenty that a grocery list will solve. "I do not spill out riches and success for the hope of a tithe and offering. I am not here to obey your every whim."

The Lord says that He is not here to ease your guilty conscience. Confession is good for the soul, but it is not a payment so you can go on sinning. "I am here as your God so that you can follow Me, obey Me and worship Me. You cannot demand My blessing."

The Lord says that He will judge you and not the other way around. "I am the Alpha and Omega and you

are only the iota in the alphabet in life. Without Me you think there is no meaning, you are finite and dust and you are lost. Without Me, you waste your breath with meaningless words and empty gestures."
"Without Me, there is no church, no chance of peace, no hope of the Resurrection and no reason to strive for the good of mankind. If I lift My hand from this world, it will be no more. Not because I will it, but as you will it."

    Does this not sound more like the times we live in? Do we not hear the thunder in heaven pealing doom to the insurrectionists who promise eternity with God? For a penny they cry out your future will be successful, hand you a plastic cross draped over by a cloth so no one can see. Leaders of men hide from the love of God vowing to guarantee success and damnation for a few cents a day.

    Even churches will resurrect the dead for a dollar, bring the vision of the Lord for ten dollars and everlasting life for twenty. All this for the love of God.

The churches are beginning to talk of a wide road to heaven and all can go there. The wide road is a carnival for religious masters who deceive us with the myth all men and women go to heaven.

> "Enter through the narrow gate. For wide is the gate and broad is the road that leads to destruction, and many enter through it. But small is the gate and narrow the road that leads to life, and only a few find it."
>
> Matthew 7: 13,14

The applause mesmerizes the lost who do not understand the difference between the reality of God and the religious fantasy that comforts those who refuse to kneel. Those who follow the lie believe all things are great and nothing is small in their cathedrals of spirits walking through the halls of graves.

How do we know we are worthy? Who says we are saved except those who lead us astray for the love of God? Who says the road is narrow? That no one would be lost? Who said few would pass into the gates? Who? The Lord our God.

Few hear the tolling of the bells until it is too late. Those that are true suffer greatly under the banner of ISIS. Under the banner of liberals. Under the banner of the evil that hates Christ and His followers.

Now back to the title of this chapter Christianity is not for cowards. We are on the brink of our own self-destruction because of sloth, laziness, cowardice, greed, self-righteousness and self-destruction. We have lost our path to God, self-reliance, capitalistic adventure, intelligence and a driving force to succeed.

What fools have conquered our nation that we must kneel to an idol of want and need? When do we stop shaking our fist at God and kneel before Him. How did we get a pro-Muslim administration that seems to acknowledges Allah over God?

Even Pope Francis has taken steps to embrace Islam, atheists and agnostics toward a one world religion. Though Christians are beheaded and burned alive by Muslims, the Pope says it is not a violent faith. Though the Koran preaches that all men and women must bow to Allah, the Pope feels it is not a danger to Christianity.

The Koran calls for violence against those who will not come to the Muslim faith. There are rumors that Pope Francis has made a deal with them to keep his head on. Like Obama, Pope Francis believes that the terrorists are only a "little fundamentalist group" He equated Catholic domestic violence with the beheading of children and Christians.

Pope Francis equated Islam and Christianity sharing "the idea of conquest." Unbelievably, Pope Francis quoted as saying "It is true that the idea of conquest is inherent in the soul of Islam. However, it is also possible to interpret the objective on Matthew's gospel where Jesus sends His disciples to all nations, in terms of the same idea of conquest."

"Then I saw three evil spirits that looked like frogs; they came out of the mouth of the dragon, out of the mouth of the beast and out of the mouth of the false prophet."

Rev. 16: 13

Are we being privy to the days of the false prophet? Is this Pope turning his back on the faith out of convenience? Fear? Political expedience? I do not believe, listening to the Pope, that he thinks Jesus is the only way, truth and life.

Democrats have shown fear of men and women who profess through faith in Christ. Our President has shown allegiance to Islam more than Christianity. As his presidency ends, Obama has openly professed his dislike for this country by trying to bankrupt its finances, its faith and its constitution.

At the democratic convention the American Flag was not flown till the end. It was burned outside the convention center. There was a cry for Bernie Sanders who was a known socialist that minimizes Christianity and upholds humanism.

Politicians on both sides use their faith to co-op votes instead of making a commitment to God. Many in this country now thing Christianity is dangerous and closed-minded.

If they did not believe this then why take our Christian heritage and historical facts from the schools? Why has the Satanic Temple been allowed to distribute its material for their cause to young impressionable children? Such a place like Orange County, Florida have seen pamphlets that read "Jesus is dead" and "Why I am not Muslim." Coloring books featuring Pentagrams, Damian and Cerberus (hound of hell).

Satanic Temple plans a Black Mass on Harvard University campus. They will display goat-headed Baphomet statue next to the Ten Commandments at the Oklahoma State Capital and now going to Detroit,

Michigan. There are Satanic Temples in Pittsburgh, Seattle and Los Angeles.

The Military Religious Freedom Foundation claim chaplains use Christianity "as a weapon to intimidate, menace, harass, subdue and terrify their otherwise helpless armed forces subordinates."

MRFF calls Christians in military "monsters who terrorize." They compared them to jihadists and demand Christian generals to be court martialed for their faith.

The story from Liberals seem to claim that if you are not perfect, you are not a true Christian, you have no say in politics or society. What they don't understand is that it is the imperfection that stands for our claim to salvation. Being perfect brings intolerance which is not the Lord's way to bring those who sin to His heart.

How is any other faith more tolerable to those who have none? What future do we have if we believe only in ourselves? Why do we seek the darkness instead of the light? Is it because it is easy to hide in the dark than the light? A shadow creeps over our nation and no one wants to carry a flashlight.

Chapter Eighteen

Political Correctness Gone Wild

    A man comes up to me and says he's a bum. Do I correct him and tell him he's just homeless? If unemployed, hapless bad luck? If you mention God, do you have to include Buddha, Allah, others? If guns kill people, do spoons make us fat? Should words be banned because they cause wars, insults and lethal misunderstandings? Should food be banned because some of them cause heart attacks, diabetes and various other illnesses? Should we ban mosquitoes because they carry disease? Where does it end?

Inanimate objects can do nothing without the will of man.

How many of us do things that only you and God know about? How hard is it to keep silent because you want others to know your good and bad deeds? It is our nature to want to be recognized for those things we have successfully accomplished.

We yearn to be embraced by those who ignored you before the act of kindness or greatness. You want others to look up to you only to realize you really wanted to look down on them. It is hard to have a happy medium for we are human and want to be loved.

We feel the love of God is not enough especially when our situation changes little when we come to Christ. Jesus asks "to pick up the Cross and follow Me." What part of the Cross do you not understand? For the Cross represents a harder life as well as a fulfilling life. Through the Cross we shall see Heaven. Through the

Cross the Spirit will lift us up through the pain into the ecstasy of eternal life.

It would be wonderful if being a Christian makes life a time of few problems and heartaches. Unfortunately, the trials and tribulations seem to increase. The stress builds until we think "Why me, Lord?" We are not forced by God to a certain future, but allowed by God to choose through an uncertain future.

>So if nothing else, remember this:
>
>"Judas, are you betraying the Son of Man with a kiss?"
>
>>Luke 22: 48

This is who we are.

>"Father, forgive them, for they know not what they do."
>
>>Luke 23: 34

This is who He is.

> "I am the way the truth and the life. No one comes to the Father except through Me. If you really knew Me, you would know my Father as well. From now on, you do know him and have seen Him."
>
> John 14; 6.7

This is what should be. Listen or be heard from no more. This is not a time for negotiations for the Lord becomes impatient with disrespect and dishonoring his name. Who would you rather have on your side? This is the time to decide for we are in the last days as scripture tells us. Oh yes, that's right, many of you don't read the scriptures. Many of you have no idea of the fulfillment of Revelation. May God be merciful to us all. Pray for everyone because everyone needs it even though everyone won't listen.

Made in the USA
Charleston, SC
20 August 2016